CELEBRATE ROSÉ

ASHLEY ROSE CONWAY
OF CRAFT & COCKTAILS

weldon**owen**

Contents

Roses & Rosé

Seaside Picnic

WHY ROSÉ COCKTAILS?

A glass of rosé is great on its own on a warm summer day, but this style of wine works well in cocktails too. Rosé is an underrated element for cocktails—it can enhance a drink with the flavorful floral and citrus notes that many drinks beg for. Sure, we have the viral darling Frosé (which you can get a recipe for on page 51), but there are still not enough recipes utilizing these pink wines. *Celebrate Rosé* is here to change that. From spritzes to twists on classics to original concoctions, you'll find rosé in every recipe in this book. And, since rosé is also a food-friendly wine, you will find pairing suggestions on page 17. Rosé is not complicated, and it doesn't take itself too seriously. Embrace the joie de vivre of rosé!

Today's rosé is not your mom or grandma's pink wine of yesteryear. As was the case in the cocktail world, the 1970s through the early 2000s were not kind to rosé's reputation. Saccharine vin and cocktails were slung about with frivolous abandon. The decline in the quality of pink wines can be pinpointed to an inaptly named White Zinfandel, the one our mothers often kept a box of in case of emergencies. It was what everyone assumed rosé was and all it could be. About ten years ago, there was a climactic shift in the demand for and production of rosé. Producers began to think about terroir revealing itself in their rosés, a sense of place that had previously been reserved for reds and whites. More effort and thought went into making delicious pink wines for our glass—and now for our cocktails. Rosés is now the comeback kid of the wine world. Rather than being picked last for dodgeball, it is now a standout sought for shelves and wine lists. There are so many fantastic labels on the market now, rosé has found itself a respected wine again. Rosé is here to stay.

This resurgence, and our growing obsession with pink wine *(what self-respecting eating establishment is not carrying at least one—or five—rosés?)*, has a little to do with the "millennial pink" color craze and a lot to do with the fact that this wine is oh-so delicious. Rosé can be paired with almost anything and is extremely quaffable. With tasting notes like melon, rose, grapefruit peel, and strawberries, plus its affordability, it's easy to see why people clamor for bottles during spring and summer, and now fall and winter too. It's just as delicious poolside as it is tableside. And who doesn't want to live the #roséallday lifestyle? You *can* have rosé all day with the delicious cocktails in the following chapters. Vive la rosé!

RUNDOWN ON ROSÉ

How Pink Wine Is Made Although some innocent souls may think there is a pink grape, that isn't the case; rosé comes from red grapes. There is no single designated rosé grape. It can be made from a variety of varietals such as Pinot Noir, Syrah, and even Cabernet Sauvignon, giving us an array of pink wine styles. Tart, acidic grapes are often used for rosé, whereas the juicier, more vibrant grapes are saved for red wine. Acidity can make a chilled rosé sing and render the wine perfect for pairing with food. Although it originated in France, rosé can be made anywhere in the world. In fact, you are likely to find at least one rosé in almost any wine-growing region around the world.

Different styles of rosé are created using one of several methods:

Saignée This method for making rosé follows the same initial step used for producing red wine—red grapes are lightly pressed—but the grape juice is "bled off" ("saignée") early in the fermentation process. Whereas red wines would continue the full fermentation with the skins, rosé spends the rest of the time fermenting without contact with the skins. Red grape skins add not only color, but also body, fruit notes, and tannins to a wine. With longer grape skin contact early on, more tannins are contributed to the rosé's overall profile. This method results in some sassy rosés.

Short Maceration Another way of creating rosé involves crushing grapes with the skins and allowing them to soak for a few hours before straining the juice. Whereas the skins soak longer to create red wine, here the grape skins have minimal contact before fermentation to get just enough flavor from them. This method commonly produces the peachy, pale rosés that are associated with the southern French region of Provence, where this method is prevalent.

Direct Press A slow pressing of grapes is used in this rosé-making method. The lengthy pressing time allows the grape skins to give the wine their color and characteristics without further maceration.

Blending Put the red in the white and drink 'em both up! Although this sounds like an ideal, easy way to make rosé—red plus white equals pink, after all—it does not always mean great results. This method is generally frowned upon when it comes to still rosés. However, for sparkling rosé, blending is the preferred method used in Champagne, the French region known for its master blenders. The red wine lends intense fruit flavors and deeper color to the final product.

Red & White Co-ferment In this method for making rosé, red and white grapes are fermented together rather than blended later. This produces a wildly different wine than just blending red and white.

MIXING IT UP

Rosé & Spirits Together Mixing with rosé is relatively easy, but it does require a bit of know-how to produce a fantastic cocktail. Developing a new recipe always includes some trial and error, and concocting a new cocktail is no different, but at least it is a delicious process.

Because some rosés lean toward being lighter bodied, their nuances can be lost in cocktails. For cocktails, try to use bright, vibrant rosés with lots of character. I like fruit-forward pink wines with fresh strawberry and ripe melon or floral notes that show off well amongst spirits and juices. There are even some rosés, often coastal ones, that shine with notes of salinity—a characteristic that makes a drink pop. I always think cocktails can do with a bit of seasoning; salt brings out fruit's sweetness, after all. These saline styles would be perfect in drinks like the Rosé Margarita (page 70).

Still rosé is the one that started the pink wine craze, but try to think outside the bottle when it comes to cocktails. Sparkling rosés add beautiful effervescence and can stand up well in mixed drinks. Lillet produces a rosé expression of their aperitif wine that adds a skosh of bitterness that some drinks beg for. There are rosé ciders, and even rosé-infused spirits like vodka, that have popped up in recent years.

A Word on Syrups For recipes that would just feel watered down with added liquid from rosé—like a frozen drink or those topped with soda water—I use a rosé syrup (page 138). Adding the rosé in syrup form lets the wine's characteristics shine through nicely while still keeping the cocktail perfectly balanced.

In general, syrups are an ideal way of adding a sweetener to cocktails. Syrups are simply a mixture of the sweetening agent (sugar, honey, or agave, for example) and water to create a liquid that can be blended into cocktails more smoothly than granulated sugar or thick honey.

Syrups are also a great way to introduce surprising and welcome flavors into a drink. They can be infused with flowers, spices, fruits, and other flavorings to change a cocktail's profile. Turn to page 138 for a complete selection of delicious homemade syrups to try.

SERVING IT UP

Tools for Mixing & Shaking Cocktails
A few essential tools are all you need to make a great drink. Of course, there are other tools to elevate your drink making, such as a sous-vide for preparing syrups and an atomizer for spritzing absinthe, but those are not necessary for the recipes in this book. Grab the tools pictured here to expertly craft the cocktails featured in this book. Although tools do not a good cocktail shaker make, they certainly lend a helping hand.

Shaker When you're blending ingredients for a cocktail that contains juices, egg whites, and other non-boozy ingredients, you can't really do without a good shaker. I prefer to use a Boston shaker. It holds up to vigorous shaking, then comes apart with a simple light tap of your palm near the middle. A three-piece cobbler shaker can get stuck and trap your cocktail inside until all the ice has melted and the drink has to be dumped. Whomp. Tin-on-tin Boston shakers are more durable than glass versions, which have a chance of breaking. Use with a Hawthorne strainer (plus a tea strainer for a double-strain).

Mixing Glass When you make booze-on-booze cocktails without fruit, syrups, or egg whites, a mixing glass is the best way to mix up your drinks. Stirring creates fewer bubbles and a smoother texture, which is ideal for this style of drink. Use with a barspoon and julep strainer.

Tea Strainer When muddled fruit and fresh herbs are used, you will need to double-strain your drink. The tea strainer is paired with the Hawthorne strainer to catch all of the small solids in the shaker.

Julep Strainer A julep strainer goes hand-in-hand with the mixing glass. It has small holes dotting the strainer that let the liquid through but catch ice chunks that would otherwise ruin the drink.

Barspoon These long spoons are used with a mixing glass to stir drinks. They can also help get cherries out of jars or place garnishes precisely on top of drinks.

Citrus Peeler To get a beautiful citrus zest, sans bitter white pith, this is the way to go. I prefer a Y peeler for its comfort and ease. It's shaped like, well, the letter Y. A channel knife will also give you a peel in a long thin coil (see page 41) if that is what you are looking for.

Square Ice Molds Generic fridge ice has its time and place, but it is not in cocktails. I mix and sip my drink with 1-inch (2.5-cm) cubes, or 2-inch (5-cm) cubes for old-fashioneds (and similar drinks).

Jigger This will be your most-used tool. Whether making a stirred or shaken drink, you will need this small double-ended cup to measure your ingredients properly. Cocktails are a science, so being a ½ or even a ¼ ounce off with the measurements can throw off your whole drink. Jiggers come in different measurement sizes, so before making your drinks be sure that you know what you've got. I prefer to mix with bell-shaped jiggers—I like their curvy shape and the way they fit in my hand. They typically hold 1 ounce on one side and 2 ounces on the other, with graduated markings on the inside for ¼, ½, and ¾ ounces.

Hawthorne Strainer Used with a cocktail shaker, a Hawthorne strainer has a spring coil that holds back ice and thicker ingredients as you pour. If you have muddled fresh herbs and fruit in your shaker, you will use this along with a tea strainer to do a double-strain.

Wine Opener Although some great wines come with screw caps these days, you will still need a wine opener for a lot of bottles of rosé. I have a few: one electric for when I am lazy, a wine key with a foil cutter that's very practical, and a wooden vintage opener for when I want to look fancy-schmancy. I always keep an opener in my purse, because you never know if you are going to save the day when people forget an opener and it stands in the way of their drinking a delicious bottle of wine!

ROSÉ FOOD PAIRINGS

Rosé, in my opinion, can go with just about any food, from briny oysters, fresh seafood, and grilled veggies to barbecue and even a juicy steak. Because it sits somewhere between a red and white wine, pink wine's characteristics can pair with a plethora of dishes. It is one of the most versatile wine styles around; it's the little black dress of the wine world!

Rosé styles range from crisp, light, and acidic to full, fruit-forward, and big bodied. Not all rosés are made the same, so you'll want to be sure to pair the right ones with your dishes. Thinner, bright styles of rosé go swimmingly with seafood and vegetables, much like a crisp white wine does. Fuller-bodied pinks made from varietals like Syrah and Cab Sauvignon go with heartier dishes like casseroles, chilies, and red meat. The following are pairings I especially love, and I hope they guide you in how to marry your rosé with a tasty bite.

Light-Bodied Rosé Pairings

Oysters are a given; serve them up with a rosé mignonette sauce

Grilled spicy or citrus shrimp

Smoked salmon toasts with dill

Roasted chicken with bread stuffing and dried currants

Baja fish tacos

A More Fruit-Forward Dry Rosé

Veggie Vietnamese spring rolls with peanut sauce. (I add edible flowers to mine for an extra-pretty touch.)

Vegetable tart with tomatoes

Spicy Thai food such as curry and papaya salad

Mussels in white wine–butter broth or tomato broth

Seafood paella

Fried chicken

Fuller-Bodied Rosé Pairings

Vegetable chili

Tzatziki sauce with grilled skewers of chicken or lamb

Grilled pork or chicken sausage

Peking duck or roasted duck with citrus sauce

Pulled pork

BOTTLE TALK

Wine preferences are as personal as a Spotify playlist. Everyone's are different and fine-tuned to their own tastes. That being said, I want to share a selection of my favorite rosés in the hope that it helps guide you in discovering your favorites. Some will sing to you, while others will feel flat, but I guarantee you will fall in love with at least one of the pink wines below.

I live in the heart of California's wine country, but I enjoy rosé from producers around the world. California and French rosés are often easier to find in your local grocery store, but don't be afraid to do a little searching to find a good bottle from a producer in Spain, Australia, Argentina, or even Hungary. Some bottles listed below are more accessible than others, but should not be too hard to find or have shipped to you in the U.S.

Sparkling Rosé

Domaine Carneros Brut Rosé
(Carneros, California)

Iron Horse Brut Rosé
(Sonoma County, California)

J Vineyards Brut Rosé
(Sonoma County, California)

Laurent-Perrier Cuvée Rosé Brut
(Champagne, France)

Moët & Chandon Rosé Impérial
(Champagne, France)

Mumm Brut Rosé (Champagne, France)
& Mumm Napa Brut Rosé (Napa Valley,
California)

Pierre-Jouet Blason Rosé
(Champagne, France)

Ruinart Brut Rosé (Champagne, France)

Santa Margherita Sparkling Rosé
(Veneto, Italy)

Schramsburg Brut Rosé
(North Coast, California)

Veuve Clicquot Ponsardin Rosé
(Champagne, France)

Still Rosé

Ameztoi "Rubentis" Rosé Getariako Txakolina (Basque region, Spain)

Banshee Rosé (Mendocino County, California)

Broc Cellars Love Rosé (California)

Charles & Charles Rosé (Columbia Valley, Washington)

Chateau Miraval Côtes de Provence Rosé (Provence, France)

Copain Tous Ensemble (Mendocino County, California)

Day Owl California Rosé

De Bortoli La Bohème Act Two Dry Pinot Noir Rosé (Yarra Valley, Australia)

Domaine de Triennes Rosé (Provence, France)

Dúzsi Tamás Kekfrankos Rosé (Hungary)

Finca Wölffer Rosé (Argentina)

Idlewild The Flower, Flora & Fauna Rosé (Mendocino County, California)

Las Jaras Mendocino County Rosé

Les Maîtres Vignerons de La Vidaubanaise Le Provençal Côtes de Provence Rosé (Provence, France)

Lieu Dit Rosé of Pinot Noir (Santa Rita Hills, California)

Matthiasson Rosé (Napa Valley, California)

Maysara Sparkling Pinot Noir Rosé (Oregon)

Railsback Frères Rosé 'Les Rascasses' (Santa Ynez Valley, California)

Reeve Rosé of Pinot Noir (Mendocino County, California)

Terrassen Rosé (Finger Lakes, New York)

Très Chic Rosé (Sud de France)

VML Rosé of Pinot Noir (Sonoma County, California)

Ladies' Night In

ASHLEY'S TIP
To keep the drinks and conversations flowing all night long, have a drink station on a bar cart or credenza within reach of your guests' seats rather than in the kitchen.

Treat your favorite ladies to an intimate night in over cocktails. Skip the buzzy restaurants and busy bars and instead invite your best friends to your place to catch up in comfort. I find evenings like these to be more meaningful and enjoyable than going out on the town anyway.

Whether there are two or ten coming over, make the night special with your own touches. Serve up a signature dish or drink, or have them leave with a favor that they can savor later and remember the evening by. If you need time to cook while guests are over, a batched cocktail like Strawberry Rosé Punch (page 43) allows for guests to serve themselves. However, if you are looking to show off your cocktail-making skills, mix up cocktails à la minute like the Rosé Vesper (page 26) or Passion Fruit–Fig Whiskey Sour (page 29).

When it comes to hosting, I want everything *juuust* perfect. But anytime I have been at someone's house and they point out something that's missing, I had never even noticed! Moral of the story: Keep It Simple Sistah. A cheese plate and charcuterie board can be just as impressive as a formal table and coursed meal among good company. Just make sure the wine and drinks are flowing and the music is setting the mode for the evening, and you are golden.

Vineyard Clover Club

SERVES 1

The traditional clover club cocktail hails from Philadelphia, just like me. Okay, okay, I am from New Jersey, but close enough! Philly is vibrant with sass and this cocktail reflects that. Silky egg whites mingle with raspberries and the botanicals in the gin, with a tart snap from the lemon cutting through any sweetness. The addition of rosé adds more berry notes without disturbing the sweet and tart balance.

¾ oz (20 ml) Simple Syrup (page 138)

6–8 raspberries

1½ oz (45 ml) gin

½ oz (15 ml) rosé with raspberry or strawberry notes

½ oz (15 ml) fresh lemon juice

1 medium egg white

GARNISH

3 raspberries

dried raspberries (optional)

Chill a coupe glass and prepare simple syrup. In a shaker, combine berries, gin, and measured-out simple syrup. Muddle berries. Strain out the solids and pour the liquid back into the shaker. Add rosé, lemon juice, and egg white. Dry shake without ice for a good 30 seconds. Add ice and wet shake for 10 seconds longer. Strain into the chilled coupe glass without ice. Garnish with raspberries. If desired, crush dried raspberries and dust over the top of the frothy drink.

Rosé Vesper

SERVES 1

—————————— 🍸 ——————————

Vespers are a classic cocktail that a certain fictional spy was very fond of. Vespers closely share their DNA with the martini. They call for a mixture of gin and vodka (yes, both!) along with the aperitif wine Lillet in place of dry vermouth. Here, I swapped out regular Lillet Blanc with Lillet Rosé. A little more fruit-forward and a vibrant pink, it provides a subtle twist that I love. Although 007 did something right by giving us the vesper, he did get one thing wrong: Martinis should never be shaken. Tiny ice shards and lots of air bubbles permeate martinis that are shaken, and I find this ruins the drink. I'll have mine with Lillet Rosé, stirred not shaken.

2 oz (60 ml) citrus-forward gin (I use Bluecoat Gin)
1 oz (30 ml) vodka
½ oz (15 ml) Lillet Rosé

GARNISH
lemon peel for expressing
lemon twist

Chill a coupe or martini glass. In a mixing glass filled three-quarters of the way with ice, combine gin, vodka, and Lillet. With a barspoon, stir for 30 seconds. Using a julep strainer, strain into the chilled coupe glass without ice. Express a strip of lemon peel over the glass, then add a lemon twist as a garnish.

Passion Fruit–Fig Whiskey Sour

SERVES 1

Fresh figs have the most delicious flavor that dried figs can't quite touch. They have two short seasons each year, so if you simply cannot get fresh figs, use rehydrated dried figs instead. Bursting with berry notes and hints of honey, figs go smashingly well with nutty amontillado sherry. Tart passion fruit plays well with bourbon, and all combined make for a intensely flavorful drink. With this cocktail in hand, you'll wanna get figgy with it!

1 fresh or rehydrated dried fig

1¼ oz (35 ml) bourbon

1 oz (30 ml) rosé

1 oz (30 ml) amontillado sherry

¾ oz (20 ml) passion fruit syrup (I use Small Hands brand)

½ oz (15 ml) fresh lemon juice

GARNISH
lemon twist
fig slice

Chill a Nick & Nora or coupe glass. Combine fig and bourbon in a shaker, and muddle. Add the rosé, sherry, passion fruit syrup, lemon juice, and ice, and shake. Using a Hawthorne strainer and tea strainer, double-strain into the chilled coupe glass without ice. Express a lemon twist over the glass and add as a garnish along with a fig slice.

Tablescape
EASY ELEGANCE

COLOR IMPACT

I like to keep the color palette simple for the decor of my dinner parties, with neutrals like white, black, and grays plus a muted accent color like peach. I then add pizzazz with vibrant floral arrangements that can be changed to fit my mood and the occasion, without having to buy all new linens for each party.

POWER OF FLOWERS

Even a simple floral arrangement can liven up the decor. I always like to have one living element on a table, whether a single impactful bloom in a vase, a garland, or a fresh-cut branch with blossoms on it. Fillers like eucalyptus, leaves, and other greenery are inexpensive and will create a canvas for colorful stems. With large blooms such as peonies, ranunculus, poppies, or garden roses, a little goes a long way in arrangements—meaning you don't need dozens of them to make a statement.

KEEP IT PERSONAL

If you are pulling out all the stops for a glamorous evening with your favorite ladies, keep a few things in mind. Make sure that any floral arrangements are low profile and don't block views across the table. Speaking from experience as a short girl, I often find it hard to make out the faces of my fellow guests through the foliage. Small arrangements or ones that creep along the table (like garlands) are the perfect option to keep guests engaged with one another.

SERVE UP SIMPLICITY

For a casual get-together with only appetizers on the menu, spread platters throughout your space to encourage guests to move around. For formal gatherings, you can keep it simple by serving family-style rather than as a coursed meal. Guests will interact more and it saves time. Pre-batch the cocktails you'll need for the evening; then all you'll have to do is pour from a pitcher, leaving you at leisure to enjoy the conversation.

Rosé Pisco Sour

SERVES 1

The addition of rosé adds a fruity but dry note to the pisco sour, a South American favorite. Pisco is a grape-based spirit, an unaged brandy from Peru and Chile. To add a great texture to the cocktail (a.k.a. mouthfeel, in cocktail speak), gum syrup will do the trick. This sweetened syrup thickened with guar gum adds a dense viscosity to cocktails. If you cannot find gum syrup, just substitute an equal amount of simple syrup in its place.

1¾ oz (50 ml) pisco (I use Macchu Pisco)

1 oz (30 ml) rosé

¾ oz (20 ml) fresh lime juice

¾ oz (20 ml) gum syrup or Simple Syrup (page 138)

1 egg white

GARNISH

3 dashes Angostura bitters

Chill a coupe or rocks glass. In a shaker, combine the pisco, rosé, lime juice, gum syrup, and egg white. Dry shake without ice. Add ice and wet shake. Strain into the chilled glass without ice. Dash bitters on top of the foam.

ASHLEY'S TIP
A heart design on top of the egg white is beautiful and easy to create. Add a few drops of dark aromatic bitters like Angostura in a row on the egg white. Insert a toothpick into the egg white starting above one of the dots of bitters, then drag the egg white through each dot in one swipe.

BOTTLED COCKTAIL FAVOR

Giving bottled cocktails or homemade spirits as party favors is a fantastic way to make a party memorable. Whip up a batch of your signature cocktail or a homemade liqueur like Rosé Limoncello (page 36) and pour into take-home bottles. Set out the bottled cocktails at each place setting with a pretty label that adds to the table decor. Guests will be delighted to take home the bottles and remember the party fondly as they sip their custom drinks. You will need: card stock, glass bottles with corks or screw tops, a hole punch, and twine.

DIRECTIONS

On a computer, use fonts or your own custom design to make a label naming the cocktail or spirit. Print out onto the card stock and cut out the labels (my ideal size for the label is 2 by 1½ inches / 5 by 4 cm). Alternatively, you can hand-letter each label directly on the cardstock for a personal touch.

Fill bottles with your custom drink.

Punch a hole through the top of each label. Thread twine through the holes and tie a label to the neck of each bottle.

Rosé Limoncello

SERVES 6

Limoncello, a traditional liqueur hailing from Italy, is the perfect after-dinner sipper. When chilled, it turns into liquid dessert: citrusy and silky, with just the right amount of kick after a heavy meal. Vibrant Almalfi Coast citrus peels steeped in a neutral spirit for a few weeks with some sugar added at the end to mellow the flavor produces a celebratory spirit to sip at leisure. I like to make a batch of this a month before the holidays to bottle up as gifts or use in bottled cocktail favors (page 34). It's liquid gold—or, in this case, rose gold!

12 organic lemons (4 lemon peels per cup of vodka)
1 bottle (750 ml) 100-proof vodka

1½ cups (350 ml) rosé
2 cups (400 g) sugar
1 cup (240 ml) water

Using a sharp vegetable peeler, zest lemons, removing the colored portion of the peels but avoiding the bitter white pith. Pour vodka and rosé into a bottle larger than 750 ml. Add lemon zest to the bottle. Set aside in a dark place for 2–3 weeks.

Pour limoncello mixture into a large bowl, straining out lemon zest, and add sugar. Stir well. Stir periodically for a few hours to incorporate sugar fully. Add water to the bowl and stir. Pour the Rosé Limoncello into 250-ml bottles if giving as gifts, or pour into two 750-ml bottles to store indefinitely.

ASHLEY'S TIP

If you can find them, use Meyer lemons to make the limoncello. They are a cousin of the everyday Eureka lemons we are accustomed to. Meyer lemons have an intoxicating smell and sweet, floral notes that make the limoncello sing, and they pair beautifully with the rosé.

Elderflower Mojito

SERVES 1

St-Germain adds a sweet, floral note that plays well with herbaceous mint. It is made from the elderflower, which lends a sweet, floral aroma with familiar peach and lychee notes to any drink. The rosé takes the place here of some of the soda water you'd use in a classic mojito, giving the drink more flavor. Be sure to muddle the mint only gently, as overmuddled mint will taste earthy and muddy the drink.

½ oz (15 ml) Rosé Syrup (page 138)

12 mint leaves

2 oz (60 ml) white rum

½ oz (15 ml) St-Germain Elderflower Liqueur

1 oz (30 ml) soda water

GARNISH

large mint sprig

elderflowers or other edible flower

Prepare rosé syrup. In a highball glass, muddle mint gently. Add rum, elderflower, and measured-out rosé syrup. Add ice to the glass. Top with soda water and stir. Smack mint sprig on glass and add as a garnish, along with flowers.

Rosé 75

SERVES 1

⸻ 🍸 ⸻

This is a pink take on the classic French champagne cocktail. With only four ingredients and no infusions required, this sparkling concoction is perfect for when you need a drink in a jiffy to serve guests. You can even pre-batch a round of these cocktails a few hours before the party. Just chill the strained drink until ready to serve, add to flutes, and pour in the bubbles for the welcome drink as guests arrive.

¾ oz (20 ml) Simple Syrup (page 138)

1½ oz (45 ml) gin (I use Monkey 47)

¾ oz (20 ml) fresh lemon juice

3 oz (90 ml) sparkling rosé

GARNISH
flakes of edible gold leaf
lemon twist

Prepare simple syrup. Drape edible gold leaf on a champagne flute.

Combine gin, lemon juice, and measured-out simple syrup in a shaker with ice. Shake, then strain into the flute. Top with sparkling rosé and stir. Express a lemon twist over the glass and add as a garnish.

ASHLEY'S TIP
Edible gold is sold in sheets online and at baking-supply stores. It is delicate and clings to moisture. Use a clean, dry paint brush to transfer the gold leaf to the glasses for an easy way to make drinks at your party shine.

Strawberry Rosé Punch

SERVES 8–10

——————————— ☕ ———————————

This grapefruit and strawberry drink for a crowd is bright and refreshing. Cocchi Americano, an aperitif wine that contains an element called quinine that gives tonic water its bitter flavor, adds interesting dimension to this drink. Serve this pretty punch in your favorite punch bowl and let your guests serve themselves while you mingle. With jewel-like garnishes, it becomes a statement piece presented on a bar cart, buffet, or table.

ASHLEY'S TIP
To keep ice from melting too fast and watering down your beautiful punch, freeze a large block of ice instead of using a lot of smaller cubes. You can use a small cooler, a Bundt pan, or other container that fits the punch bowl circumference. The larger the surface area of the ice, the slower the ice melts. I told you cocktails were science!

4½ oz (130 ml) Simple Syrup (page 138)

6 oz (180 ml) Cocchi Americano

6 strawberries

4½ oz (130 ml) fresh lemon juice

1 bottle (750 ml) rosé

6 oz (180 ml) grapefruit juice

6 oz (180 ml) grapefruit soda

GARNISH

ice block or ring

½ grapefruit, sliced

1 lemon, sliced

4 strawberries, sliced

handful of mint leaves

handful of edible flowers

Prepare simple syrup. In a shaker, combine Cocchi Americano, 6 strawberries, lemon juice, and measured-out simple syrup. Muddle, then shake with ice. Using a Hawthorne strainer and tea strainer, double-strain the muddled mixture into a punch bowl with an ice block or ring. Add rosé, grapefruit juice, and grapefruit soda to the bowl and stir. Garnish with fresh fruit slices, mint leaves, and edible flowers. Serve with a ladle into punch glasses.

Rooftop Fête

Throwing a rooftop party has a special charm to it. Nestled between the cityscape and sky, a rooftop offers sweeping views—a stunning backdrop for enchanting conversations. As the sun sets, twinkling lights and golden reflections on the buildings make for a beautiful show.

Rooftops are city dwellers' answer to a lack of backyards. I like to think of my roof as the patio I never had. Rooftop and porch parties are also fantastic for small-space dwellers. Rather than jamming your friends and neighbors into your already-cramped studio apartment, set up your favorite spread on the roof. Treat these outdoor spots as an extended space for entertaining friends and loved ones.

Serving up a selection of easy-to-prepare snacks along with the right cocktails means you can set the patio party on autopilot and enjoy. Mix up the Sunday Funday Sangria (page 64), a make-ahead crowd-pleaser, or the surprisingly sophisticated Sugar, Honey Honey (page 52), which I always find goes down almost too easy. With the perfect drinks, fabulous company, and sky-high views, your rooftop fête will be *magnifique!*

Rosé Gin & Tonic

SERVES 1

Gin and tonics have been a staple in my family for as long as I can remember. Thanks to the Spanish, G and Ts have evolved from a quaint English two-ingredient drink into a beautiful bouquet of spices, herbs, and fruit. The clear drink displays these colorful ingredients like jewels, which is fitting as spices used to be worth more than gold. Luckily, we can drop them into our gin and tonics with abandon.

2 oz (60 ml) gin (I use
Four Pillars Dry Gin)

1½ oz (45 ml) Lillet Rosé

4 oz (120 ml) tonic water
(I use Q Indian Tonic)

GARNISH

flower ice (page 109)

rosemary sprig

grapefruit slice

10 juniper berries or pink
peppercorns

Prepare flower ice cubes and place in a chilled wineglass. Smack rosemary sprig on glass and add as a garnish, along with a grapefruit slice and peppercorns. Pour in gin and Lillet Rosé. Top with tonic water. Stir with a barspoon, and enjoy.

ASHLEY'S TIP
Pink peppercorns are actually a type of small, dried berry. When you bite into them, they pop with a peppery spice, then finish with a floral berry flavor. You can find them in some grocery stores, health-food stores, and online. Use their unique flavor profile groundin salt rims, simmered in syrups, or infused into spirits.

Amaro Frosé

SERVES 4

Y

This is not your average frosé. It's still a lovable blushing pink slushy, but with more depth to it than the typical recipes that are floating around, which can often be one-note and saccharine. I add amaro to the mix to give it balance and dimension while still keeping it recognizable with strawberry, lemon, and, of course, the key ingredient in this Instagram darling, rosé. The amaro adds a touch of bitterness and backbone to this frozen drink.

32 oz (950 ml) rosé

3 oz (90 ml) fresh lemon juice

5 oz (150 ml) simple syrup (page 139)

14 frozen strawberries (about 1 lb/450 g)

7 oz (210 ml) Amaro Montenegro or Aperol

2 oz (60 ml) vodka

GARNISH

4 lemon twists

4 strawberries

4 edible flowers

Distribute rosé and lemon juice into ice cube trays and freeze, in batches if needed. Prepare simple syrup.

Once the liquids are frozen, combine them with the remaining ingredients in a blender. Blend well. Scoop into glasses. Express a lemon twist over each glass and add as a garnish, along with a strawberry and an edible flower.

Sugar, Honey Honey

SERNES 1

▮

Although they are sweet, apples have a tart snap to them that forms a winning combo when combined with oaky bourbon. Sugar, in one form or another (liqueur, honey, or simple syrup), is vital to a cocktail, but I prefer my cocktails well balanced and not too sweet. Honey is the perfect addition to create depth of flavor while adding a subtle sweetness.

¾ oz (20 ml) Honey Syrup (page 139)

3 oz (90 ml) Honeycrisp apple juice, or other red apple juice

1½ oz (45 ml) bourbon (I use Russell's Reserve 10 Year)

1 oz (30 ml) rosé

¼ oz (7.5 ml) fresh lemon juice

4 dashes bitters

GARNISH

crushed ice

rosemary sprig

apple slices

Prepare honey syrup. In a shaker, combine apple juice, bourbon, rosé, measured-out honey syrup, lemon juice, bitters, and ice. Shake and strain into a highball glass with crushed ice. Smack rosemary sprig on glass and add as a garnish, along with apple slices.

Tablescape
ROOFTOP SOIREE

GET CREATIVE

Sophisticated does not have to mean complicated. If the rooftop is hard to access or you do not have patio furniture available, a long portable card table with a thick linen table-cloth layered over it will look chic. Adorn it with wooden serving pieces, marble trays, greens like eucalyptus, and colorful napkins to create a stunning setting for a festive party.

PRETTY PAPER

Keep things super simple! Instead of ceramic plates, use paper plates. Before you scoff and close this book, know that paper plates have come a long way. I love all of the stylish options on the market from places like Harlow & Grey and Oh Happy Day. They have wonderfully creative designs and patterns that will add to any party's decor.

LET IT SHINE

It can be challenging to haul a whole meal to the roof, but thankfully summer produce doesn't require a lot of fuss to shine. Make-ahead salads, bruschetta, and cheese plates are ideal dishes that do not need much cooking. Who wants to be slaving over a hot stove in the middle of the summer?

YES WAY CRUDITÉ

Bring back those crudités platters! Crudités do not have to be boring or flavorless. Here's my advice for a great crudités platter: two or three different dips, a creamy cheese for dipping fruit into (such as burrata or ricotta drizzled with honey), vegetables that taste good raw (buh-bye broccoli and celery), a variety of colors and textures, and making sure each piece is easy to eat in one or two bites—eliminating the dreaded double dip.

WHEN I DIP, YOU DIP

Speaking of dips, skip the ranch. Instead opt for an unexpected option like green goddess or tzatziki. If you have a grill, you cannot go wrong serving skewers of lamb, chicken, or veggies to dip. This will still keep things simple while adding a warm option to the table.

The French Rose

SERVES 1

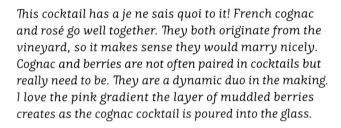

This cocktail has a je ne sais quoi to it! French cognac and rosé go well together. They both originate from the vineyard, so it makes sense they would marry nicely. Cognac and berries are not often paired in cocktails but really need to be. They are a dynamic duo in the making. I love the pink gradient the layer of muddled berries creates as the cognac cocktail is poured into the glass.

¾ oz (20 ml) Rose Syrup (page 138)

4 blackberries

6 raspberries

1¼ oz (35 ml) cognac or aged grape brandy

¾ oz (20 ml) rosé

½ oz (15 ml) fresh lemon juice

GARNISH

large ice cube

mint sprig

blackberries

edible flowers

Prepare rose syrup. In a rocks glass or small stemmed glass, muddle blackberries. In a shaker, muddle raspberries. Add the cognac, rosé, measured-out rose syrup, and lemon juice to the shaker, along with ice, and shake.

Place a large ice cube in the serving glass with the blackberries. Using a Hawthorne strainer and tea strainer, slowly double-strain the cocktail into the glass. Smack mint sprig on glass and add as a garnish, along with more berries and, if desired, edible flowers.

ASHLEY'S TIP
True cognac is a French brandy produced in the Cognac region. Much like true champagne, it has to come from its region of origin and be produced in the traditional method to be labeled as such. The French take their booze seriously. I like their style! In place of cognac, a non-French aged grape brandy like Copper & Kings will also work here.

DIY
CHAMPAGNE TOWER

Nothing quite says celebration like a champagne tower! Often reserved for New Year's Eve and weddings, this party trick makes a glamorous statement at your next soiree. Champagne towers are easy to assemble, but take a little know-how. Plastic coupes are the most economical and safe route, but if you do want to use real glassware, choose coupes with wide-based and thick rims that will be steady. Although not required, a tray catches a toppled tower or any champagne overflows, making cleanup easier. You will need: 1 tray with a lip, 9 plastic or glass coupe glasses, 2 bottles rosé champagne or sparkling wine, and flowers (optional).

DIRECTIONS

Place the tray on a stable surface.

Form the base of the tower. The first layer will have 5 glasses. Arrange 4 of them in a square. Add the fifth one between two of the glasses, forming a pentagon. Make sure the glasses' rims are touching one another; the next layer will be balancing on the rims.

Add the next layer of glasses. Take 3 coupes and balance them on top of the other coupes, making sure their rims touch one another in the center.

Add the last glass on top in the center of the 3 coupes.

Tuck flowers around the tower, balancing them on the glass rims.

Pour champagne into the top coupe slowly. Let it over flow into the next layers of glasses until all of the coupes are filled with the bubbly.

Rosé & Bitters

SERVES 1

I

Soda and bitters are a great little hair of the dog. I tend to need a bit more of a kick in my ailment the next day, so I add in sparkling wine, which won't leave me with a hangover part two. The bitters lend a lot of flavor to the bubbles, making it feel like a hearty cocktail when in fact it's a low-ABV sipper. One of these after a little too much fun the night before will revive you.

¼ oz (7.5 ml) Simple Syrup (page 138)

4 oz (120 ml) sparkling rosé

2 oz (60 ml) soda water

6–8 dashes aromatic bitters (I use Angostura)

GARNISH

orange twist

Prepare simple syrup. Fill a collins glass with ice. Add sparkling rosé, soda water, and measured-out simple syrup to the glass and use a barspoon to stir. Dash bitters over the top. Express an orange twist over the glass and use as a garnish. Stir bitters before sipping.

ASHLEY'S TIP
There are a lot of bitters on the market currently and new flavors are added every day, it seems. Feel free to experiment with different bitters in place of the Angostura to find your favorite combination in this bubbly cocktail.

Watermelon Raspberry Rosé Granita

SERVES 6

ASHLEY'S TIP
To take the granita to the next level, turn it into a parfait layered with homemade vanilla whipped cream, a grating of lemon zest, and a garnish of berries and a mint sprig.

Granitas are a fabulous icy treat for a warm day. They are way less complicated to make than ice cream or sorbet, but just as cool and satisfying. I made this granita boozy with rosé in place of the water normally used in the recipe. The rosé is not cooked out of this dessert, which means it has a kick. If kids are present at the party, be sure to warn everyone of the potency of this frozen treat.

2 cups (480 ml) rosé
5 cups (760 g) diced watermelon
1¼ cups (250 g) sugar
1 cup (120 g) raspberries
1½ Tbsp fresh lime juice

GARNISH
6 lime twists
6 watermelon wedges
6 raspberries

Combine rosé, watermelon, sugar, raspberries, and lime juice in a blender and blend until smooth. Pass through a fine-mesh strainer into a baking pan or similar container, and place in the freezer. After 3–4 hours, start scraping the granita with a fork to encourage ice crystals to form, and to fluff it. Repeat this scraping every hour until the granita is completely frozen. To serve, scoop into cocktail glasses or sorbet bowls, garnish with lime twists, watermelon wedges, and raspberries, and enjoy with a spoon.

Sunday Funday Rosé Sangria

SERVES 6

This is a sangria to serve on a Sunday to forget all about Monday. Don't let the pink hue and fruit cocktail fool you: this potion can be sneaky. Aside from rosé, it's laced with brandy and orange liqueur. As with any sangria, the magic happens while it rests before serving. The fruit infuses more and more flavor into the cocktail the longer it sets. If you have time, infuse for 24 hours before serving. Should you be in a hurry to get the sangria into people's hands, four hours should do. No Sunday Funday would be complete without this sangria.

1 bottle (750 ml) rosé
4 oz (120 ml) brandy
2 oz (60 ml) Cointreau or other orange liqueur
3 oz (90 ml) simple syrup
1 peach, sliced
6 strawberries, sliced
1 lemon, sliced

½ grapefruit, sliced
1 cup (240 ml) sparkling water

GARNISH
strawberries
raspberries
orange or grapefruit slices

In a pitcher, combine rosé, brandy, orange liqueur, syrup, and fruit. Stir and chill for at least 4 and up to 24 hours in the fridge. Just before serving, add sparkling water. Garnish with strawberries, raspberries, and citrus slices.

ASHLEY'S TIP

If you plan to serve this sangria at a long, leisurely brunch or to a large crowd, add an additional 1 cup (240 ml) soda and 2 oz (60 ml) simple syrup. This will stretch the sangria longer and lower the ABV (alcohol by volume) a bit for guests to sip throughout the day while still giving it a perfectly balanced taste.

Poolside Party

If you give me a chair by a pool and a glass of rosé, I will lounge there for hours. Treat your friends and yourself to a cabana-like experience in your own backyard. Putting together an inviting and serene environment lays the groundwork for the ultimate relaxing pool party.

If ever there was an ideal time to bring out my summery glassware, it's a pool day! Hurricane glasses, filled with my Rosé-lada (page 74) and garnished with pineapple leaves, evoke island getaways, while vintage tropical mugs filled to the brim with my Caribbean Cooler (page 89) recall the best of tiki escapism. Punch bowls or pitchers are also a favorite of mine to set out for guests to dip into throughout the day.

Textural pieces in summer white and natural rattan make for a clean and crisp look—summer is all about simplicity in my eyes. To engage all of the senses, I have a curated playlist ready to listen to while lounging in the sun. There is a plethora of perfect songs to choose from for a pool party to set the mood for the day. With a relaxing setting, an evocative playlist, and these refreshing cocktails, your next pool party will surely make a big splash.

Rosé Margarita

SERVES 1

You would be hard-pressed to find a cocktail more beloved, at least in the U.S., than the margarita. This quintessential agave drink single-handedly introduced tequila into the American mainstream. My go-to formula includes tequila, fresh lime juice, agave nectar, and Cointreau for orange notes to support the citrusy, tart lime. And always salt. The rosé syrup here adds more fruit notes that marry with the orange liqueur while taking the place of the agave for sweetness. A coastal rosé with some salinity to it works really well for this drink.

½ oz (15 ml) Rosé Syrup
(page 138)
2 oz (60 ml) tequila (I use
Partida Blanco)
1 oz (30 ml) fresh lime
juice
½ oz (15 ml) Cointreau

GARNISH
pink salt for glass rim
lime wedge for glass rim
lime wheel

Prepare rosé syrup.

Spread coarsely ground pink salt on a plate. Run a lime wedge around half the rim of a glass. Run the rim of the glass through the salt.

In a shaker, combine tequila, lime juice, Cointreau, measured-out rosé syrup, and ice. Shake and strain into the prepared glass with ice. Garnish with a lime wheel.

ASHLEY'S TIP
To salt the glass rim or not—that is the question! I am always on team salt, but I know that some people prefer their margaritas without salt. To please everyone, I salt only half the rim. That way, those who want salt can sip from the salty side, while those who do not want salt can sip from the other side.

Rosé Daiquiri

SERVES 1

Havana is the spiritual home of the daiquiri and other classic rum drinks. A simple cocktail of white rum, lime, and sugar, the daiquiri is an archetype for many cocktails. Because it is so simple, be sure to use the best ingredients you can get. Although Havana is not known for its rosé, this elegant spin-off adds a nice twist. Instead of settling for a simple lime slice, I take it up a notch with the garnish. Small clothespins corral herbs and flowers that you may not want floating in your drink.

¾ oz (20 ml) Rosé Syrup
(page 138)

2 oz (60 ml) white rum
(I use Plantation 3 Stars)

1 oz (30 ml) fresh lime
juice

GARNISH

lime slice

edible flowers

Chill a coupe glass and prepare rosé syrup. In a shaker, combine rum, lime juice, measured-out rosé syrup, and ice. Shake and strain into the chilled coupe glass without ice. Garnish with a lime slice and edible flowers.

Rosé-lada

SERVES 1

🍸

Is there any other cocktail that can transport you to a poolside cabana as quickly as a piña colada? This rosé-spiked colada adds subtle fruit flavors that support the tangy pineapple and coconut. Far from your typical cloying colada, this is a fruit-forward creamy concoction with hints of caramel from the rum that will have you singing that yacht rock song.

3 oz (90 ml) Rosé Syrup (page 138)

2 oz (60 ml) aged white rum (I use Plantation 3 Stars)

2 oz (60 ml) pineapple juice

2 oz (60 ml) coconut milk

1 oz (30 ml) coconut cream

2 cups (275 g) ice

GARNISH
pineapple leaves
pineapple wedge
edible flower

Prepare rosé syrup. In a blender, combine rum, pineapple juice, coconut milk and cream, measured-out rosé syrup, and measured-out ice. Blend until smooth. Pour into a hurricane glass, tiki mug, or highball glass and garnish with pineapple leaves, a pineapple wedge, and an edible flower.

Tablescape
MAKE A SPLASH

COCO CABANA

Create a cabana experience in your own backyard. A comfy space where everyone can relax in between dips in the pool can be curated with ease with just a few things. Colorful poufs and pillows are perfect for reclining while you dry off. A side table holds cocktails while also setting a focal point to gather around. Baskets for towels will keep things corralled and neat around the pool. This will all instantly transform the pool deck into a luxe lounge.

BAR CART

Bar carts are not just for indoor entertaining—you can wheel your bar out to bring the party outside! Stock the mobile bar with everything you'll need for the day so you won't have to run indoors constantly for supplies. Having everything at hand will give you more pool and rosé time. Things to keep in mind to add to the bar cart—besides the drinks, of course—include napkins, shakers, strainers, glassware, an ice bucket, a bottle opener, and tiki umbrellas (a must for a pool party)!

SATURATED HUES

I tend to stick to neutral colors (blush is a neutral), but when it comes to pool parties, I like to go for more than just a splash of color. Saturated coral, cerulean, and teal are my go-to hues for poolside parties. If you want to add in a pattern for a pop of whimsy, go for a large print in only one to two colors to keep from being too busy. Finished off with pops of green from palm fronds and plants, your pool will feel like a remote tropical oasis.

FLOAT ON

Cool, kitschy floats have become staples at pools everywhere. Who wouldn't want to spend their day floating on a giant inflated flamingo while getting some sun? I totally lean into floats and the rosé-all-day lifestyle at the pool. Not all floats come with a cup holder, though, so if you or your friends are looking to imbibe while you float your cares away, make sure to get one that can hold your beverage, too.

Rosé Swizzle

SERVES 1

▌

Swizzle it, just a little bit! Swizzled drinks are just as fun to make as they are to drink. Okay, almost as fun. Built in the glass, swizzles use specially shaped wooden (or plastic or metal) sticks called swizzle sticks (hence the name). Swizzle sticks swirl and agitate the crushed ice to chill the cocktail down quickly. This swizzle is a take on the Queen's Park Swizzle. It's minimalist, but packed with lots of flavor. I swapped in Plantation Pineapple rum, which is my desert island spirit—I would happily drink only this for the rest of my life if I had to.

¾ oz (20 ml) Rosé Syrup (page 138)

8 mint leaves

2 oz (60 ml) Plantation Pineapple Rum or a Demerara rum

1 oz (30 ml) fresh lime juice

8 dashes Angostura bitters

GARNISH
crushed ice

mint sprig

pineapple leaves

Prepare rosé syrup. In a highball glass, gently muddle mint leaves. Add crushed ice to fill the glass. Add rum, lime juice, and measured-out rosé syrup. Insert a swizzle stick or a barspoon and twist and swizzle it back and forth until frost begins to form on the glass.

Add more crushed ice to dome over the rim of the glass. Dash bitters on top. Smack mint sprig on glass and add it as a garnish, along with pineapple leaves.

DIY
FRINGE TIKI UMBRELLAS

I make custom piñatas for parties when I am not shaking cocktails, so I often have crepe paper lying around. I had an idea to take some leftover strips of fringe from the piñata and add it to a cocktail umbrella, which just so happened to be in the drink I was sipping. Now I have some of these on hand at all times to garnish my tropical drinks. Come to think of it, it would be the perfect topper to any drink, really. Every cocktail deserves a little flair! You will need: ½ by 35-inch (12 mm by 90-cm) strips of crepe paper or tissue paper in colors of your choice, scissors, cocktail umbrellas, hot glue, and hot glue gun.

DIRECTIONS

Cut crepe or tissue paper into ½ by 35-inch (12 mm by 90-cm) strips, going against the grain on crepe paper.

On one side, cut fringe along the length of the paper, cutting with the grain if using crepe paper. Cut the fringe only halfway through to the other side.

Starting at the bottom edge of the drink umbrella, glue the strip with the hot glue and adhere it to the tiki umbrella.

Spiral the fringe up the umbrella as you glue, being sure to overlap the layers below.

Finish off the fringe at the tip of the umbrella with a bit of glue, cutting off any excess fringe.

Just Peachy

SERVES 1

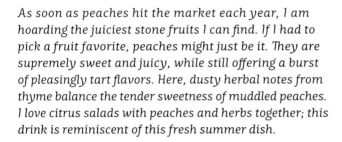

As soon as peaches hit the market each year, I am hoarding the juiciest stone fruits I can find. If I had to pick a fruit favorite, peaches might just be it. They are supremely sweet and juicy, while still offering a burst of pleasingly tart flavors. Here, dusty herbal notes from thyme balance the tender sweetness of muddled peaches. I love citrus salads with peaches and herbs together; this drink is reminiscent of this fresh summer dish.

½ oz (15 ml) Simple Syrup (page 139)

4–5 peach slices

1¾ oz (50 ml) aged Jamaican rum (I use Appleton 12 year)

½ oz (15 ml) rosé

½ oz (15 ml) fresh lemon juice

1 thyme sprig

GARNISH

thyme sprig

peach slices

Prepare simple syrup. In a shaker, muddle peaches well. Add rum, rosé, lemon juice, measured-out simple syrup, thyme, and ice. Shake and double-strain into a rocks glass with ice. Smack a thyme sprig on the glass and add as a garnish, along with peach slices.

The Smoky Melon

SERVES 1

Even before I tested this recipe, I knew that it would be an instant hit! It features mezcal, which is a beautiful earthy and smoky spirit produced from the agave plant. Tequila, widely loved, is actually a type of mezcal. Mezcal is particularly pleasant when paired with ripe, sweet melons that aid in taming its smokiness. If smoky spirits are not your jam, however, feel free to replace the mezcal with your favorite tequila.

¾ oz (20 ml) Rosé Syrup (page 139)

2 oz (60 ml) watermelon juice, or 1 cup (150 g) cubed watermelon

1 oz (30 ml) cantaloupe juice, or 1 cup (150 g) cubed cantaloupe

2 oz (60 ml) rosé

1¾ oz (50 ml) mezcal (I use Del Maguey)

¾ oz (20 ml) fresh lime juice

Pinch of salt

GARNISH

mint sprig

cantaloupe cubes

Prepare rosé syrup. If not using melon juice, in a shaker, combine watermelon and cantaloupe cubes (in batches as needed) and muddle well. Strain out the solids and return the melon juices to the shaker. Add the rosé, mezcal, measured-out rosé syrup, lime juice, salt, and ice. Shake and double-strain into a wineglass with ice. Smack mint sprig on glass and add as a garnish, along with cantaloupe cubes.

ASHLEY'S TIP
Ice is a key component in cocktails and shouldn't be overlooked. It chills and dilutes simultaneously while it's being shaken or stirred; we would have awfully subpar cocktails without it. Store your ice in a sealed bag or container in the freezer to prevent smells from permeating it and ruining your perfectly crafted cocktail.

Patio Pounder Punch

SERVES 16

ASHLEY'S TIP
Along with a large block of ice, frozen fruit help keep a punch chilled for a longer period. Chill your garnish grapes and cucumber slices before adding them to a punch, to keep things extra icy on a sweltering hot day. Frozen grapes also make a great snack!

This punch is immensely refreshing and easy to drink—a guaranteed crowd-pleaser. Cooling cucumber, kiwi, and grapes mingle harmoniously with herbaceous mint and botanical gin here. You will want to sip this after a long day of swimming or while sitting on the patio with a few good friends as the sun fades into the horizon. Although it contains quite a few ingredients, nearly everything hits the blender, making this a breeze to whip up.

8 oz (240 ml) Simple Syrup (page 139)

20 oz (600 ml) gin (I use St. George Spirits Botanivore)

20 oz (600 ml) earthy or herbal rosé

8 oz (240 ml) fresh lime juice

8 kiwis, peeled

4 cups (600 g) green grapes

3 green apples, cored and sliced

2 cucumbers, chopped

32 mint leaves

12 oz (350 ml) ginger beer

GARNISH

ice block or ring

mint leaves

white grapes

cucumber slices

lime slices

kiwi slices

Prepare simple syrup. In a blender, combine the gin, rosé, measured-out simple syrup, lime juice, kiwis, grapes, apples, cucumbers, and mint leaves. Blend. Pour through a strainer into a medium-sized punch bowl, discarding the solids. Top with ginger beer. Stir and add ice block or ring. Garnish with mint, grapes, and cucumber, lime, and kiwi slices.

Caribbean Cooler

SERVES 2

❚

Sipping tiki drinks is an essential poolside activity, but they can have an exorbitant amount of sugar in them. Enter my Caribbean Cooler! It's built on the tiki archetype—a couple of rums layered with citrus juices, tropical fruits, and some baking spices for zing—but it's also fresh-tasting and balanced, truly a drink that is greater than the sum of its parts. A splash of sparkling rosé adds unexpected bubbles that make this drink sing.

1½ oz (45 ml) Cinnamon Syrup (page 139)

6 oz (180 ml) pineapple juice

3½ oz (105 ml) grapefruit juice

3 oz (90 ml) white rum (I use Plantation 3 Stars)

1 oz (30 ml) aged rum (I use Appleton Reserve)

2½ oz (75 ml) sparkling rosé

GARNISH

crushed ice

nutmeg

tropical fruit such as starfruit or pineapple

orange peel

edible flowers

Prepare cinnamon syrup. In a shaker, combine fruit juices, rums, measured-out cinnamon syrup, and ice. Shake and strain into a tiki mug or highball glass with crushed ice. Top with sparkling rosé and more crushed ice. Grate nutmeg on top. Garnish with tropical fruits and orange peel. (I roll my orange peel starting from one end to form a rose.)

ASHLEY'S TIP
Use fresh juice in your cocktails whenever possible. The difference between fresh and bottled juices is like night and day. I strain my freshly pressed juices before shaking with them to remove any remnants of pulp that would otherwise muddy the drink.

Roses
& Rosé

Invite your favorite people over for a lovely afternoon gathered in the garden! A garden party doesn't require living on an estate with sweeping grounds. Billowing flower arrangements, draping garlands, and floral headpieces can create a lush garden atmosphere in any backyard.

A garden is the ideal setting for a stylish party. Cookouts are a favorite of mine, but sometimes I want something more elegant and intimate. Party-sized pitchers of floral libations like the Lillet Basil Smash (page 94) and the Flower Fields Fizz (page 109) are on theme and will be sure to get the party blooming. Finger food, chilled dishes, and floral cocktails create an effortless but delicious spread.

Lighting may not be the first thing on your mind when planning an outdoor event, but for a garden party, the right lighting can really set the mood. For a gathering that will continue well past the sunset, flickering candles and dramatic shadows create a romantic, cozy setting to end the evening with. By day, the candlesticks will add height and dimension to the tablescape. Similarly, a dainty string of fairy lights overhead creates a magical space for friends and family to share.

Lillet Basil Smash

SERVES 1

The smash's simple architecture of spirit, citrus, and muddled herbs and fruit served over ice leaves lots of room for creative variations. The Lillet Basil Smash is particularly smashing, blending rosé, sweet and tart grapefruit, and peppery basil. I use classic white Lillet here for a subtle bitter quality that dances across the palate with the sweet and tart grapefruit. While I am usually partial to gin when I need a clear spirit, here I choose vodka—it hangs back unannounced while other ingredients take center stage.

½ oz (15 ml) Simple Syrup (page 138)

6 basil leaves

1 oz (30 ml) vodka (I use Hangar 1)

1½ oz (45 ml) rosé

1¼ oz (35 ml) red grape-fruit juice

½ oz (15 ml) Lillet Blanc

GARNISH

basil sprig

Chill a coupe glass and prepare simple syrup. In a shaker, gently muddle basil leaves. Add vodka, rosé, grapefruit juice, Lillet, and measured-out simple syrup, along with ice. Shake and double-strain into the chilled coupe glass without ice. Smack basil sprig on glass and add as a garnish.

A Rosé by Any Other Name

SERVES 1

In this dainty drink, a flower petal rim adds a subtle floral note, while honey syrup adds an earthy, rich flavor that regular sugar syrup cannot. You may feel apprehensive at first about using egg whites in your drinks, but once you mix one up in your cocktail, you won't go back! Egg whites add a silken, almost creamy texture that rounds out the tart acidity from the citrus. Dry shake the egg white without ice first to whip it.

1 oz (30 ml) Honey Syrup (page 139)

1½ oz (45 ml) gin (I use St. George Spirits Botanivore)

1 oz (30 ml) rosé

1½ oz (45 ml) fresh lemon juice

1 medium egg white

4 drops rose water (optional)

GARNISH

sugar for glass rim

edible flowers such as dried fresh rose petals and lavender buds

Prepare honey syrup and measure out 1 oz (30 ml).

Scatter 2 Tbsp sugar on a small plate. Mix 1–2 tsp chopped edible flowers into the sugar. Wet the rim of a coupe glass and roll into the flower mixture.

Combine gin, rosé, lemon juice, honey syrup, and egg white in a shaker. Dry shake without ice until the mixture sounds heavy, 30–60 seconds. Add ice and wet shake for 12 seconds. Strain into the prepared coupe without ice. Sprinkle with rose water, if using, and additional flowers.

ASHLEY'S TIP
Rose water is an ingredient often used in Middle Eastern cooking. You can find it in natural-foods stores or online. It can be very intense, so be sure not to go overboard here— just use a few drops in the drink.

What's the Tea Old-Fashioned

SERVES 1

ASHLEY'S TIP
No heat is needed to steep the tea here. Alcohol is a great solvent and will pull out the flavor from anything added to it. Because of this, be careful not to overinfuse when using strong flavorings such as spices and hot peppers like jalapeños.

What's the Tea is an homage to a cocktail from my favorite, now closed, neighborhood haunt—Two Sisters Bar & Books in San Francisco—called the Chamomile Old-Fashioned. It was beloved by many in the city. This is the ideal drink for curling up with a good book or for sipping on while spilling tea with your bestie.

½ oz (15 ml) Honey Syrup (page 139)

1¾ oz (50 ml) Chamomile Bourbon (page 139)

¾ oz (20 ml) rosé

2 dashes aromatic bitters (I use Angostura)

GARNISH

large ice cube

lemon twist

chamomile flowers

Prepare honey syrup and chamomile bourbon. In a mixing glass, combine measured-out chamomile bourbon, rosé, measured-out honey syrup, and bitters. With a barspoon, stir for 30 seconds. Strain into a teacup or old-fashioned glass with a large ice cube. Express a lemon twist over the glass and add as a garnish, along with chamomile flowers.

Tablescape
ALFRESCO IN THE FLOWERS

IN BLOOM

In spring and summer, every flower imaginable is in season; even fruit trees and herbs are bursting with colorful buds. I tend to take elements of my dishes and drinks, whether a color or an ingredient, and weave them throughout the decor. Bright berries, roses, and flowering herbs mixed into the cocktails can also be mirrored in the tablescape. Herbs, citrus branches, and edible flowers make stunning flower arrangements and can also work well for place settings. It makes the whole party cohesive down to the last petal.

A TOUCH OF VELVET

A simple tablecloth gets elevated with a sumptuous velvet table runner. Velvet is often tucked away until the winter holidays, but I like to bring it out and create dramatic moments throughout the whole year. I use it sparingly in spring and summer tablescapes, selecting just one small accent, such as a table runner or napkins.

ROSE-COLORED GLASSES

Break out your prettiest glasses to instantly upgrade any outdoor dinner party. I bought a set of pink Depression-glass goblets for my wedding that are my most treasured pieces to this day; they create shimmering pink reflections that whirl across the table in the sunlight.

MIX & MATCH

Alfresco entertaining is an invitation to unwind a bit. With elegant glassware and luxe linens in solid colors, you can mix textures, patterns, and even different styles of dishware to make a table look and feel eclectic. This way you also don't require a full set of matching dishes for a large party. Try melamine plates in a fun pattern in complementary colors or simple white dishes in varying textures and styles. I always love a little high brow–low brow moment that lets my guests relax rather than feeling like they have to remember which fork goes with which course.

Rosé Cobbler

SERVES 1

—————————— ▮ ——————————

ASHLEY'S TIP
Shaking with a strip of citrus zest releases oils that lend a delicious depth of flavor to your drinks. Make sure there isn't any white pith left on the zest—it will add an undesirable bitter flavor to the cocktail.

Cobblers are low-octane crushed-ice drinks that are totally crushable. They are one of the oldest recorded cocktails (from the 1830s). The straw owes its place in modern society to the cobbler cocktail, which required one to suck up every last drop from the glass full of crushed ice. Instead of plastic, choose a sustainable option when it comes to straws for your drinks—like thick paper, metal, or glass. Summer berries in this recipe can be traded in for plump pears and bright citrus come fall and winter.

¼ oz (7.5 ml) Simple Syrup (page 138)

3 oz (90 ml) amontillado sherry

2 oz (60 ml) fruit-forward rosé

¾ oz (20 ml) fresh lemon juice

5 raspberries

2 strawberries

1 strip orange zest

GARNISH

crushed ice

mint sprig

raspberries

strawberries

orange slice

Prepare simple syrup. In a shaker, combine the sherry, rosé, lemon juice, measured-out simple syrup, berries, and orange zest, and muddle the berries. Add ice and shake quickly, about 5 seconds. Using a Hawthorne strainer and tea strainer, double-strain into a collins glass or flute with crushed ice. Smack mint sprig on glass and add as garnish, along with raspberries, strawberries, and an orange slice.

DIY
BOTANICAL ICE BUCKET

You will never want to use a regular ice bucket again! This fruit- and floral-sprinkled ice bucket is easily crafted, but will make a serious statement displayed at your next party. It might be hard to decide which is cooler, the ice bucket or the rosé chilling inside. You will need: ice bucket or medium plastic bucket, plastic container ½–1 inch (12 mm–2.5 cm) smaller in circumference than the first bucket but large enough to fit a wine bottle, flowers of your choosing, and fruit slices or berries such as grapefruit, strawberries, raspberries, and herbs.

DIRECTIONS

Take the larger bucket and fill with a few inches of water. Freeze to create the base layer.

Insert the second plastic container inside the larger bucket and weigh it down.

Fill the gap between buckets halfway with water. Add half of the flowers, fruit, and herbs and place in the freezer. Let freeze completely.

Add the rest of the flowers, fruit, and herbs and fill all the way with water. Return to the freezer. When frozen, remove the smaller container, using warm water along the outside of the bucket if needed to loosen the container. Freeze the botanical ice bucket until ready to use.

To serve, place the botanical ice bucket on a shallow tray to catch melted water. Place wine or bottled cocktails in the bucket to chill.

Rosé Ramos Fizz

SERVES 1

A Ramos gin fizz is a dessert and cocktail in one. It's a velvety, creamy drink that is like a milkshake, if milkshakes were a boozy cloud. Both avoided and revered in the cocktail world, Ramos fizzes are worth the time and shaking. Rumor has it they were shaken for 10 minutes when they were first created, but you can slide by with just 3 and still have a heavenly Ramos fizz.

¾ oz (20 ml) Rosé Syrup (page 138)

2 oz (60 ml) gin

½ oz (15 ml) fresh lemon juice

½ oz (15 ml) fresh lime juice

1 medium egg white

½ oz (15 ml) heavy cream

1 oz (30 ml) soda water

GARNISH

lemon twist

Prepare rosé syrup. In a shaker, combine gin, measured-out rosé syrup, citrus juices, and egg white and dry shake without ice for 3–4 minutes. I check at 3 minutes, and if I feel I need more foam, I shake for another minute. You'll want to shake hard to get the egg white whipped. Once you have done this, add in cream and 2 regular ice cubes and shake until you don't hear any rattling—which means the ice has melted and chilled the drink. Without straining, pour cocktail into a small collins glass. Let sit for 30 seconds. Slowly pour in the soda water until the foam begins to rise above the glass. (Make sure the collins glass isn't too big, so the foam can rise above the rim.) Express a lemon twist over the glass and add as a garnish.

Flower Fields Fizz

SERVES 1

The first sip of this floral drink whisks you away to a warm spring day! I was admittedly wary of floral flavors in food and drinks for a long time. If you go overboard, your drink ends up tasting oddly familiar yet off-putting. Ah, yes, grandma's potpourri. I have come around to adding more fragrant flowers to my drinks now. A gentle hand is key when it comes to flowery ingredients, unless it's an edible flower garnish—then, use liberally! Layering elderflower liqueur and lavender syrup adds dimension to this spritzer without creating a perfume bomb.

½ oz (15 ml) Lavender Syrup (page 139)

1½ oz (45 ml) rosé

1¼ oz (35 ml) vodka

½ oz (15 ml) St-Germain Elderflower Liqueur

1¼ oz (35 ml) fresh grapefruit juice

1 oz (30 ml) club soda

GARNISH

flower ice cubes (see Tip)

lavender sprig

grapefruit peel

Prepare the lavender syrup. In a shaker, combine rosé, vodka, elderflower, measured-out lavender syrup, and grapefruit juice and shake for 10 seconds. Strain into a highball or collins glass with rose ice. Top with club soda and stir. Smack lavender sprig on glass and add as a garnish, along with a grapefruit peel.

Spiked Agua de Jamaica

SERVES 2–4

Agua de jamaica is a nonalcoholic hibiscus iced tea enjoyed all over Mexico. It is made in pitchers at home and can also be found alongside jugs of horchata at roadside stands and markets as a refreshing reliever on a sweltering day. Hibiscus flowers add both a subtle floral flavor along with a tart, almost citrus, quality to drinks. This recipe will make two 8-oz (240-ml) servings or four 4-oz (120-ml) servings.

1 cup (240 ml) Hibiscus Tea (page 139)

4 oz (120 ml) rosé

2 oz (60 ml) tequila

1 oz (30 ml) fresh lime juice

1–2 hibiscus flowers

1 lime or lemon slice

GARNISH

hibiscus flowers

lemon or lime slices

Prepare hibiscus tea. In a small pitcher, combine sweetened tea, rosé, tequila, and lime juice. Add hibiscus flowers and lime slice. Chill before serving. Pour tea in glasses with ice to serve. Garnish with additional hibiscus flowers and citrus slices.

Prim & Proper Pimm's Cup

SERVES 10

ASHLEY'S TIP
If you are not a fan of ginger, swap out the ginger beer for a good grapefruit soda or fruit-flavored sparkling water like strawberry or lemon.

Pimm's was created by an oyster-bar owner in the mid 1800s, no doubt as a pairing for his bivalves. A secret mash-up of herbs and fruit dance throughout this gin liqueur, making it equally complex and refreshing. Ginger beer or soda water lengthens the spirit into a favorite summer sipper called a Pimm's Cup. Sparkling pink wine in place of some of the ginger beer really makes this perfect for brunch as well as an evening aperitif. Serve alongside oysters with rosé mignonette as an homage to the inventor of this quaffable liqueur.

5 oz (150 ml) Simple Syrup (page 138)

23 oz (680 ml) Pimm's #1

5 oz (150 ml) fresh lemon juice

12½ oz (370 ml) sparkling rosé

15 oz (445 ml) ginger beer

GARNISH

mint sprig

cucumber slices

strawberry slices

orange slices

lemon slices

Prepare simple syrup. In a pitcher, combine the Pimm's, lemon juice, and measured-out simple syrup. Stir well and add ice. Top with sparkling rosé and ginger beer and stir gently. Serve in highball glasses with ice. Smack mint sprig on glass and add as a garnish, along with cucumber, strawberry, orange, and lemon slices.

Seaside Picnic

For a delightful daytime gathering, bring the party to the beach. There is nothing quite like the warm sun on your face and the sound of the rolling waves to make stress melt away immediately. And a glass or two of rosé doesn't hurt either! If you ask me, rosé was made for a leisurely beach picnic.

One of my favorite features of a beach party is that there is no need to cook! Some of my most-loved foods are fabulous for the beach: charcuterie boards and fresh-shucked briny oysters require little to no prep. Handheld items like tacos can be ordered from your favorite restaurant ahead of time. Just toss the take-out boxes and arrange the food on a pretty tray, and it will feel homemade.

Instead of bringing beach beers and wine, I mix up big-batch cocktails, or, for a last-minute gathering, I bring supplies for the perfect bubbly summer drink, Rosé Aperol Spritz (page 136), which comes together in seconds. Preparing individual cocktails at the beach or park can be cumbersome, so leave your shaker at home. Just prep one of these drinks ahead of time—try the Rosé Sunset (page 127) or Blueberry Sage Collins (page 131)—dig your toes in the sand, and let the worries drift away.

Watermelon Paloma

SERVES 1

The margarita may be a menu staple at many American cantinas, but a paloma is the tequila beverage everyone in Mexico reaches for. Tart grapefruit can come in the form of fresh juice or as grapefruit soda. Adding in watermelon juice adds another refreshing component to this tall drink. And if you have ever added salt to your watermelon, you'll know what a fascinating flavor contrast they make.

½ oz (15 ml) Rosé Syrup (page 138)

2 oz (60 ml) watermelon juice, blended from ½ cup (75 g) diced watermelon

2 oz (60 ml) tequila

1¼ oz (35 ml) fresh grapefruit juice

1 oz (30 ml) soda water

GARNISH
coarse salt for glass rim
lime wedge for glass rim
watermelon slice or grapefruit slice

Prepare rosé syrup.

Spread coarse salt on a plate. Run a lime wedge around half the rim of a highball glass (or in whatever pattern you desire), then run the rim of the glass through the salt.

In a shaker, combine watermelon juice, tequila, grapefruit juice, measured-out rosé syrup, and ice. Shake and strain into the prepared glass with ice. Top with soda water. Garnish with watermelon or grapefruit slices.

ASHLEY'S TIP
To get the ombré effect shown in the cocktail here, add watermelon juice and rosé syrup to the salt-rimmed glass with ice first. Pour the rest of the ingredients slowly into the glass. Stir before serving.

Strawberry-Mint Bourbon Shrub

SERVES 1

ASHLEY'S TIP
In autumn and winter, replace the white wine vinegar in the shrub with apple cider vinegar or even balsamic vinegar to add a richer flavor profile to the cocktail.

In the culinary world, shrubs are fruity drinking vinegars. Dating back to Colonial times, they began as a way of preserving fresh fruit flavors into the cold, frosty months. Drinking vinegars work wonderfully in cocktails. Because of their sweet and sour balance, shrubs make for an easy drink. Top with booze—in this case rosé and bourbon— and a splash of club soda to make a drink that will having you coming back, sip after sip.

1¼ oz (35 ml) Strawberry Shrub (page 139)

1 oz (30 ml) bourbon

1½ oz (45 ml) rosé

1 oz (30 ml) club soda

GARNISH

large ice cube

mint sprig

strawberry

Prepare strawberry shrub. Put a large ice cube in a rocks glass. Add measured-out shrub, bourbon, rosé, and soda. Stir with a barspoon. Smack mint sprig on glass and add as a garnish, along with a strawberry.

Coming Up Rosé

SERVES 1

Everything is coming up roses and rosé with this drink! This fizzy sipper feels surprisingly healthy, like a wellness spa in a glass. Cucumber and rosé are a refreshing and complementary duo together in a beverage. I use Hendrick's, a cucumber-infused gin, to really drive home the crisp flavor. A citrus-forward gin like Monkey 47 will also work beautifully here.

1 oz (30 ml) Rosé Syrup
(page 138)

1½ oz (45 ml) cucumber-
or citrus-forward gin

¼ inch (6 mm) cucumber

¾ oz (20 ml) fresh lime
juice

Pinch of salt

2 oz (60 ml) sparkling rosé

GARNISH
cucumber ribbon
rose bud

Prepare rose syrup. In a shaker, combine gin and cucumber and muddle well. Add measured-out rose syrup, lime juice, salt, and ice, and shake. Using a Hawthorne strainer and tea strainer, double-strain into a highball glass with ice. Top with sparkling rosé and gently stir. Garnish with a cucumber ribbon and rose bud.

ASHLEY'S TIP
When you're making infusions and flavored syrups, always label and date the finished product; masking tape or decorative washi tape works well. I cannot tell you how many times I've grabbed a jar out of my fridge not knowing what was in it, let alone how long it had been there.

Tablescape
SEASIDE SIPS

LOUNGE BY THE SEA

Creating a comfortable lounge space will encourage hours and hours of fun at the beach. I like to bring a few thick blankets or a jute rug to keep the sand at bay and out of the food. They also create an even surface for trays, which means no spilled drinks. Placing the food and drinks in the center of the lounge space will also help keep them from getting gritty. Pretty poufs serve a dual purpose. They can be used as seating or as a low table for holding platters and trays.

OUT OF THE BLUE

Take a cue from your natural surroundings for inspiration for the decor for the picnic. Dark blues like indigo shibori-dyed blankets and pillows will integrate nicely with the backdrop of cerulean waves. Items made from natural materials, such as wooden boards for serving or woven seagrass poufs, will feel at home at the beach.

TEXTURIZE

If you want to go the extra mile and create an ambiance with flowers, keep them minimal, since you will have to haul everything onto the beach. Pampas grass, eucalyptus, and dried flowers are light and will keep all day without any water. They add texture and effortless sophistication to any picnic.

HELPING HANDS

Be sure to have an extra pair of hands to help prep and break down. If there is a lot to pack in, don't be afraid to ask for help from a friend. A wagon that can go on the beach will also help make setting up easier. After a long, fun day in the sun, having to carry twenty loads to and from the car solo would be a buzzkill.

Rosé Sunset

SERVES 1

▮

I don't know about you, but when I hear the words "tequila sunrise," it makes me cringe with regret. That was one of those drinks ordered in college that made for a not-so-pleasant sunrise the next day. I wanted to update this dive bar drink with fresh ingredients. Cheap grenadine is pure corn syrup and food dye. Thank you, next. Real pomegranate grenadine, on the other hand, is a revelation. You'll happily want to end your day with one or two of these rosé sunsets.

½ oz (15 ml) Real Grenadine Syrup (page 139)

1 oz (30 ml) tequila (I use Partida)

1 strawberry

1 oz (30 ml) fresh orange juice

½ oz (15 ml) fresh lime juice

1 oz (30 ml) sparkling rosé

GARNISH

½ strawberry

1 brandied cherry

Prepare grenadine syrup. In a shaker, combine tequila, strawberry, orange juice, and lime juice. Muddle, then shake with ice. Strain into a stemless wineglass or highball glass with ice. Top with sparkling rosé, and stir. Measure out the grenadine syrup and slowly pour into the center of the glass. Garnish with a strawberry half and a brandied cherry impaled on a cocktail pick.

ASHLEY'S TIP
Cocktails are a lot of fun and a bit of science. When layering cocktails like the Rosé Sunset, the heaviest (most often sweeter) liquids will sink to the bottom. Pour these last slowly, over the back of a spoon into the center of the glass to create a beautiful layer at the bottom. Don't forget to stir before sipping to properly balance the drink.

DIY
GRADIENT
GLASSWARE

I love to collect pretty glassware. I am constantly looking for vintage coupes and unique shapes and colors that catch my eye. When they do, they tend to come home with me. I love the gradient glassware from the '50s often called Blendo, but it can be hard to find and when I do find it, it's often pricey and never in the colors I am looking for. I decided to decorate my own for my cocktails! They take only a few minutes and you can make them in any color of the rainbow. I have made quite a few of these gradient glasses already to add to my collection (which may border on glassware-hoarder status). At least I am ready for any cocktail situation! You will need: glassware, plastic wrap, painter's tape/masking tape or Scotch tape, and nontoxic spray paint in the color of your choice.

DIRECTIONS

Lay down protective paper in a well-ventilated area.

Stretch plastic wrap over the opening of a glass, then secure with tape.

Make sure the tape is covering at least 1 inch (2.5 cm) below the lip of the glass. This will prevent anyone from ingesting any paint when drinking out of the glass.

In one hand, hold the glass upside down. With the other, hold a can of spray paint 3–4 inches (7.5–10 cm) away from the glass and even with the bottom of the glass, and spray a steady stream of paint. It should create a faded effect up the glass. If not, hold the spray paint can 4 inches (10 cm) above the glass. Rotate the glass while spraying. Taper off the spray paint towards the lip of the glass by pulling back the spray paint can slowly as you spray. Slowly work your way towards the lip of the glass and as you do, pull the spray paint can away until it creates a faded look.

Let the paint dry for a few hours, then remove the tape and plastic. Hand wash the glasses.

Blueberry Sage Collins

SERVES 1

ASHLEY'S TIP
If you are pre-batching (a.k.a. making ahead) cocktails that include soda water or sparkling wine for a party or picnic, add those ingredients in just before serving. This will preserve all of the effervescence—there is nothing worse than a bubbly cocktail that has gone flat.

A plethora of herbs both in the drink and as the garnish gives this fruity collins cocktail more complexity. Much of what we taste comes from our perception of scent (think of when you have a stuffy nose and cannot taste your food). Fragrant garnishes can be paramount to a cocktail's overall flavor. To release the fragrant oils in fresh herbs, gently smack the herbs on the side of the glass. This will give you a whiff of their herbal goodness when you go in for each sip.

6 blueberries

2 oz (60 ml) rosé

1½ oz (45 ml) gin

¾ oz (20 ml) fresh lemon juice

2 sage leaves

2 thyme sprigs

1 rosemary sprig

1 oz (30 ml) soda water

GARNISH

sage sprig

thyme sprig

rosemary sprig

blueberries

In a shaker, muddle blueberries. Add the rosé, gin, lemon juice, sage leaves, thyme sprigs, and rosemary sprig, and ice, and shake. Double-strain into a collins glass, highball glass, or footed glass with ice. Top with soda water. Smack herb sprigs on glass and add as garnishes, along with a few blueberries.

Rosé Julep

SERVES 1

∎

Bourbon-based juleps may have many a Derby lover and Southerner's hearts, but the earliest iterations of this simple minty drink were made with French brandy. Two grape-based spirits, cognac and rosé, are mixed together in this julep. If drinking a julep without bourbon in it simply won't do for you, go ahead and swap out the cognac for it in this recipe. I won't tell.

½ oz (15 ml) Simple Syrup
(page 138)
10 medium-sized mint
leaves
1¾ oz (50 ml) cognac or
aged grape brandy
¾ oz (20 ml) rosé

GARNISH
crushed ice
mint sprig
powered sugar

Prepare simple syrup. In a julep cup or rocks glass, muddle mint leaves gently. Add cognac and measured-out simple syrup and stir. Pack tightly with crushed ice. Smack mint sprig on cup and add as garnish. Dust powdered sugar over the julep.

ASHLEY'S TIP
If you do not have a fridge that crushes ice, a new, clean canvas bag and mallet will do the trick. Add ice to the bag and roll up the opening. Use the mallet to crush up the ice in the bag; the canvas will soak up any of the melted ice, and you can scoop directly from the bag into your glass. If you want to get stylish about your canvas bag and mallet, a Lewis bag kit is what you're looking for.

Orchard Shandy

SERVES 1

If you feel timid about making cocktails, this recipe is for you. It is foolproof! You don't need to reach for the shaker or mixing glass here. It is built in the glass, which sounds fancy, but it just means you dump all of the ingredients into the glass and it's ready. You got this! An elaborate garnish can elevate the straightforward drink, but a few simple slices of apple will do just as nicely.

8 oz (240 ml) dry hard cider, chilled (I use Ethic Cider Golden Rule)

1 oz (30 ml) sparkling rosé, chilled

¾ oz (20 ml) St-Germain Elderflower Liqueur

½ oz (15 ml) fresh lemon juice

2 oz (60 ml) apple juice

2 oz (60 ml) ginger beer

GARNISH
lemon twist
red apple slices
edible flowers (optional)

Make sure your cider and rosé are chilled before using. In a flute glass, combine elderflower liqueur, lemon juice, and apple juice. Stir well with a barspoon. Top with cider, sparkling rosé, and ginger beer. Gently stir again. Express a lemon twist over the glass and add as a garnish, along with apple slices and, if using, edible flowers.

ASHLEY'S TIP
Making a beautiful apple rose for a garnish takes a few steps but is worth the effort. Cut an apple in half lengthwise and use a mandolin or sharp knife to slice it very thinly. Cut the slices into half-moons and trim away the core. Soak the slices in lemon water for about an hour to make them pliable and prevent browning. Lay down the first slice. Add another slice in the same direction, overlapping about three-quarters of the previous slice. Continue this process with 6 slices. Starting from the end you began with, roll up the apples tightly. Skewer the apple through the center with a cocktail pick, if needed.

Rosé Aperol Spritz

SERVES 1

Aperol spritzes are quintessential summer sippers. They are just as good by the pool as they are at a barbecue or a picnic. They are as easy to make as 1-2-3. Their proportions are 1 part club soda, 2 parts Aperol (a bitter orange aperitif), and 3 parts sparkling wine. They do not require a shaker or mixing glass, making them a go-to for any leisurely gathering. To jazz up the basic cocktail, I've swapped out the traditional prosecco for a sparkling rosé and added a grapefruit slice in place of orange to give it a new flavor profile.

3 oz (90 ml) sparkling rosé
2 oz (60 ml) Aperol
1 oz (30 ml) club soda

GARNISH
grapefruit slice

Put ice in a wineglass and let chill. Add the rosé, Aperol, and club soda to the glass and stir. Garnish with a grapefruit slice.

ASHLEY'S TIP
Spritzes are a beloved drink in Italy. They are often served as aperitifs before a meal and come in varying flavors. To further jazz up this spritz, you can swap out the Aperol for a different aperitif liqueur or wine, such as Suze, Cocchi Americano, or—for a bracingly bitter spritz—Campari.

SYRUPS...

...and Other Flavorful Elements. *You will find syrups, shrubs, and infusions in many cocktail recipes—in both classics and modern-day libations. They are ideal ways to inject the sweetness or tartness needed to balance a drink. Syrups, shrubs, and infusions are also easy ways to infuse fascinating flavors into your drinks. Shake things up and make these cocktail recipes your own! Swap out the regular simple syrup for a flavored version in some of the recipes in this book, or add a twist to your favorite classic drink with one of these intriguing elements.*

Simple Syrup

Makes 1½ cups (350 ml)

In a saucepan over medium heat, heat 1 cup (200 g) sugar and 1 cup (240 ml) water, stirring until the sugar is dissolved. Remove from the heat. Let cool completely before using. Store in the fridge for up to 1 month.

Rosé Syrup

makes 3 cups (700 ml)

Rosé syrup allows the bright floral notes of rosé to be mixed into a drink, when too much liquid from pink wine would throw off the harmony of the ingredients, as in a Rosé Daiquiri (page 73). The rosé is not cooked out here as it is heated only slightly, so the syrup has a kick. You will find that a few of the recipes throughout *Celebrate Rosé* call for rosé syrup, but I have a feeling you will be wanting to put this in everything!

In a medium saucepan over low heat, combine 2 cups (480 ml) rosé and 2 cups (400 g) sugar. Heat and stir just long enough to incorporate the sugar into the rosé. Adding too much heat will ruin the delicate flavors of the rosé, so don't let the syrup rise past a simmer. Remove from the heat and chill before using. The syrup will keep in the fridge for few months, but use it within a few weeks for the best flavor.

Honey Syrup

makes 1½ cups (350 ml)

In a saucepan over medium heat, heat 2 cups (360 g) honey and 1 cup (240 ml) water, stirring to combine. Remove from the heat and let sit until completely cooled, about 1 hour. Strain and store in a jar in the fridge for up to a few weeks.

Lavender Simple Syrup

makes 1½ cups (350 ml)

In a saucepan over medium heat, heat 1 cup (200 g) sugar and 1 cup (240 ml) water, stirring to dissolve sugar. Add ¼ cup (7 g) lavender buds and remove from the heat. Let steep until completely cooled, about 1 hour. Strain and store in a jar in the fridge for up to a few weeks.

Real Grenadine Syrup

makes 1½ cups (350 ml)

In a saucepan over medium heat, heat 1 cup (200 g) sugar and 1 cup (240 ml) pomegranate juice (fresh if possible), stirring until the sugar is dissolved. Remove from the heat. Add 4 drops orange flower water. Let cool completely before using. Store in the fridge for up to 1 month.

Cinnamon Syrup

makes 1½ cups (350 ml)

In a saucepan over medium heat, combine 8 oz (225 g) sugar (I use demerara for more depth), 1 cup (240 ml) water, and 2 chopped-up cinnamon sticks. Bring to a simmer and let simmer for 10 minutes. Remove from heat and let cool. Strain out the cinnamon sticks. Store syrup in a jar in the fridge for up to a month.

Chamomile Bourbon

makes 1½ cups (350 ml)

Add 2 chamomile tea bags to 1½ cups (350 ml) bourbon. Let infuse for 4 hours. Remove the tea bags. Store bourbon indefinitely in a closed container at room temperature.

Hibiscus Tea

makes 1 cup (240 ml)

Bring 1 cup (240 ml) water to a boil. Add ½ cup (20 g) dried hibiscus flowers and stir. Let steep for 10 minutes. Strain out the flowers. Let cool before using in the cocktail.

Strawberry Shrub

makes 16 oz (475 ml)

In a 32-oz (950-ml) jar, combine 1 cup (150 g) sliced strawberries and 1 cup (200 g) sugar, then muddle. Cover and let sit for at least 12 hours or up to overnight, occasionally muddling. Pour ¾ cup (180 ml) white wine vinegar into the jar, cover, and shake to dissolve any remaining sugar. Strain through a fine-mesh strainer into a fresh jar. Refrigerate and let macerate for a few days or up to a few weeks before using; the vinegar bite will mellow with time. Store in the fridge to enjoy for a few months.

RESOURCES

Online

A few of these sources have shops you can visit and even sip at, but they also provide a great selection of rosés online to ship to your door.

Bottle Rocket – New York City
www.bottlerocket.com

D&M Wine and Liquors – San Francisco
www.dandm.com

Domain LA – Los Angeles
www.domainela.com

Flat Iron Wines – New York City
www.flatiron-wines.com

Frankly Wines – New York City
www.franklywines.com

Henry & Son – Minneapolis
www.shophenryandson.com

K&L Wine Merchants – San Francisco, Los Angeles, and Redwood City, California
www.klwines.com

Leon & Son – New York City
www.leonandsonwine.com

Verve Wine – New York and San Francisco
www.vervewine.com

The Wine House – Los Angeles
www.winehouse.com

Brick & Mortar Wine Shops

Bachannal – New Orleans
www.bacchanalwine.com

Fig & Thistle Market – San Francisco
www.figandthistlesf.com

Ordinare Wines – Oakland, California
www.ordinairewine.com

Red & White – Chicago
www.redandwhitechicago.com

Silver Lake Wine – Los Angeles
www.silverlakewine.com

Wine & Market – Lexington, Kentucky
www.wineandmarket.com

INDEX

Celebrate Rosé

A WELDON OWEN PRODUCTION
1045 Sansome Street
San Francisco, CA 94111
www.weldonowen.com

Library of Congress Cataloging-in-Publication
data is available.

ISBN: 978-1-68188-460-8

ACKNOWLEDGMENTS

Weldon Owen wishes to thank the following
people for their generous support in producing
this book: Lisa Berman, Lesley Bruynesteyn,
Lou Bustamante, Sarah Putnam Clegg,
and Elizabeth Parson.

FROM THE AUTHOR

I'd like to thank Lou for
the introduction and Amy,
Kelly, and Meghan for all
the hard work bringing this
book to life. Thanks to Dad
for the cocktail inspirations,
Mom who helped some of
the shoots come together
seamlessly, and to Crystal,
Tiffany, John, and Lizzie
for being there. And thank
you to Matt for being
extremely supportive and
helpful during the book
process, I could not have
done this without you!

WELDON OWEN INTERNATIONAL

President & Publisher Roger Shaw
SVP, Sales & Marketing Amy Kaneko
Associate Publisher Amy Marr
Creative Director Kelly Booth
Art Director Meghan Hildebrand
Original Design Alisha Petro
Imaging Manager Don Hill

Photography & Styling Ashley Rose Conway